Why It Matters

The Supreme Court

Liz Sonneborn

Children's Press®
An Imprint of Scholastic Inc.

Content Consultant
Saikrishna Bangalore Prakash
James Monroe Distinguished Professor of Law
Paul G. Mahoney Research Professor of Law
Miller Center Senior Fellow
University of Virginia
Charlottesville, Virginia

Teacher Adviser
Rachel Hsieh

Library of Congress Cataloging-in-Publication Data
Names: Sonneborn, Liz, author.
Title: The Supreme Court : why it matters to you / Liz Sonneborn.
Description: New York : Children's Press, An Imprint of Scholastic, Inc., 2019. | Series: A true book |
    Includes bibliographical references and index.
Identifiers: LCCN 2019012885 | ISBN 9780531231869 (library binding) | ISBN 9780531239988 (pbk.)
Subjects: LCSH: United States. Supreme Court—Juvenile literature. | Judicial power—United States—
    Juvenile literature.
Classification: LCC KF8742 .S5865 2019 | DDC 347.73/26—dc23
LC record available at https://lccn.loc.gov/2019012885

All rights reserved. Published in 2020 by Children's Press, an imprint of Scholastic Inc.
Printed in North Mankato, MN, USA 113

SCHOLASTIC, CHILDREN'S PRESS, A TRUE BOOK™, and associated logos are trademarks and/or
registered trademarks of Scholastic Inc.

Scholastic Inc., 557 Broadway, New York, NY 10012

1 2 3 4 5 6 7 8 9 10 R 29 28 27 26 25 24 23 22 21 20

**Front cover: A protest in front
of the Supreme Court
Back cover: The Supreme Court justices**

Find the Truth!

Everything you are about to read is true *except* for one of the sentences on this page.

Which one is **TRUE**?

T or F The president could nominate a kid to serve on the Supreme Court.

T or F The first female justice joined the Supreme Court in 1906.

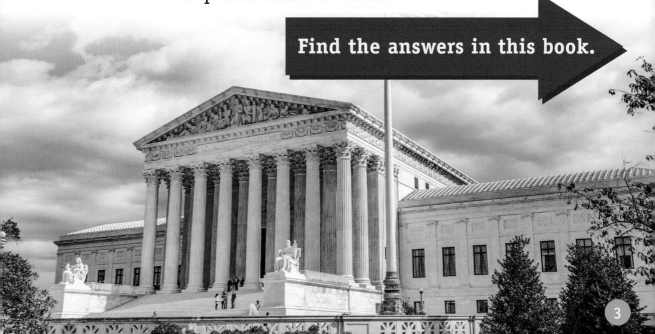

Find the answers in this book.

Contents

The BIG Truth

The Court on Camera

Justice is often represented
as a set of scales.

Saying the Pledge of Allegiance

3 The Court at Work

How do Supreme Court justices rule on a case? **27**

4 You and the Court

How do Supreme Court decisions affect you? **35**

Thurgood Marshall

Neil Gorsuch

Sonia Sotomayor

Elena Kagan

Brett Kavanaugh

Stephen Breyer

Clarence Thomas

John Roberts

Ruth Bader Ginsburg

Samuel Alito

Think About It!

What do you see in this photograph? Nine older men and women posing in black robes in front of a red velvet curtain. You've probably never met these people. A label shows each of their names. How could they have anything to do with your life? The fact is, though, they matter very much to you. As the **justices** of the Supreme Court, the decisions they make affect you and every other person in the United States.

Intrigued?
Want to know more? Turn the page!

Each year, justices have a front row seat for the president's State of the Union address to Congress.

Article III in the U.S. Constitution created the Supreme Court. The Constitution, written in 1787, sets rules for how the **federal** government works within our **republic**.

The Constitution established three branches, or parts, of the government. The legislative branch includes Congress. It makes laws that all citizens have to follow. The president heads the executive branch. This branch sees that the laws are put into practice.

The Supreme Court is part of the judicial branch and is the highest court of law in the nation. The Supreme Court has final say in deciding what a federal law means. The court can also strike down a law or a president's action by declaring it **unconstitutional**. This means the law or action goes against the Constitution. In this way, the judicial branch checks the power of the other branches. The court's decisions also directly impact you. They help determine what rights you have.

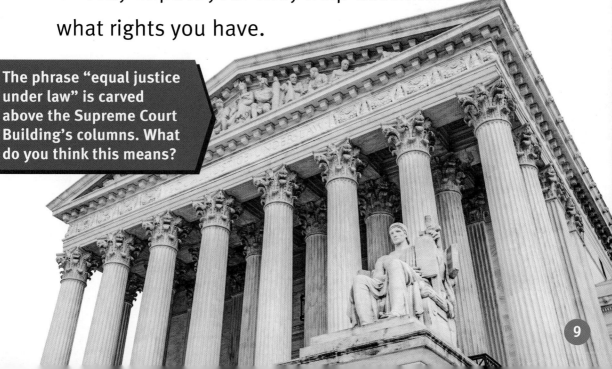

The phrase "equal justice under law" is carved above the Supreme Court Building's columns. What do you think this means?

William Taft was the only U.S. president to have served on the Supreme Court.

Sonia Sotomayor is sworn in before the hearing that determined whether she should become a member of the Supreme Court.

CHAPTER

1

Being a Justice

Since 1869, the Supreme Court has been made up of nine justices. Eight of them are associate justices. One is the chief justice. The chief justice has extra responsibilities. But when deciding cases, each justice votes on who should win, and every vote is equal.

The justices have no set term limits. They leave the court by retiring, being removed from office, or dying. Seats do not open up on the court very often. When one does, the president **nominates** a new justice.

The Right Experience

The Constitution does not have any rules for who can serve on the court. There is not even an age requirement. That means a president could nominate a kid like you to the Supreme Court!

In practice, however, presidents want to choose people who have a lot of experience with and knowledge of the law. Nearly all Supreme Court justices have been lawyers. Many have also served as judges.

Before the Senate

The Senate must approve Supreme Court nominees. Senators hold hearings to ask nominees questions about their record in the courtroom. The senators then vote on the nominees. The Senate usually approves a president's pick. If they reject the nominee, the president has to nominate someone else.

The president always hopes a new justice will support their policies. But once confirmed, justices can rule on a case however they think best.

Sometimes political opinions are said to be on the "right" or "left." The official in this cartoon is implying he wants a new justice to fill a vacancy in the Supreme Court who agrees with his right-leaning opinions. How might that benefit this official?

The Chief Justice

Some chief justices were associate justices who were promoted. But others, including the current chief justice, John Roberts, took on the job when they joined the court.

As chief justice, Roberts is the head of the entire judicial branch. He is also in charge of swearing in new presidents. If Congress wants to remove a president from office, the chief justice oversees the **impeachment** trial.

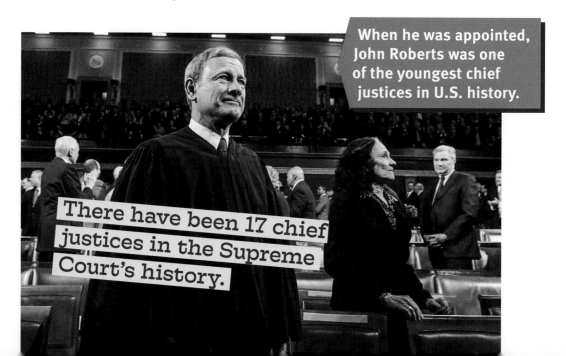

When he was appointed, John Roberts was one of the youngest chief justices in U.S. history.

There have been 17 chief justices in the Supreme Court's history.

A More Diverse Court

As of 2019, out of 114 total justices, 108 have been white men.

Thurgood Marshall was the first African American justice. President Lyndon B. Johnson nominated him in 1967. Before then, Marshall fought for the rights of black Americans during the civil rights movement. Clarence Thomas became the second African American on the court in 1991. He joined during George H. W. Bush's presidency.

Clarence Thomas served in several different government positions before he became a justice of the Supreme Court.

These are all the women who have served on the Supreme Court. From left to right, they are Sandra Day O'Connor, Sonia Sotomayor, Ruth Bader Ginsburg, and Elena Kagan.

How many years did the Supreme Court go without having a female justice? Nearly 200.

President Ronald Reagan nominated Sandra Day O'Connor, the first female justice, in 1981. Since then, three other women have taken seats on the court—Ruth Bader Ginsburg, Sonia Sotomayor, and Elena Kagan. Justice Sotomayor also became the first Hispanic person on the Supreme Court when she joined in 2009.

Justice Sonia Sotomayor is a big New York Yankees fan.

Justices for the People

Most Supreme Court justices stay out of the public eye. Justice Sonia Sotomayor, though, enjoys meeting the public. Nicknamed the People's Justice, she writes books and makes speeches to help Americans understand the court.

Justice Ruth Bader Ginsburg is another popular justice. There are several movies that tell of her career as a lawyer fighting for women's rights. Some of her fans wear T-shirts with her picture. A few even have Justice Ginsburg tattoos!

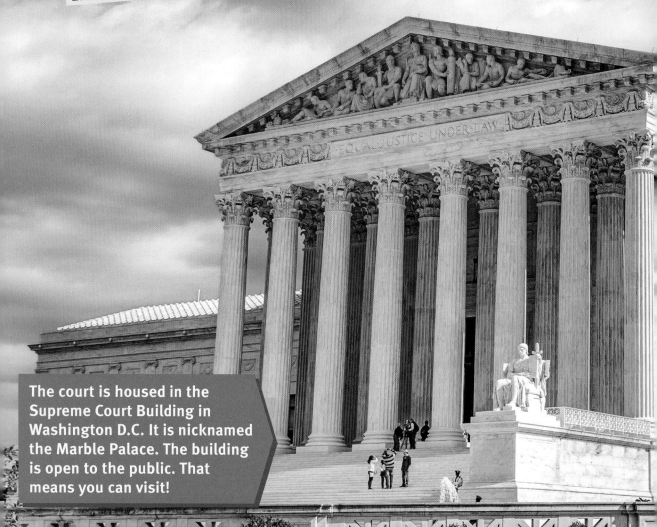

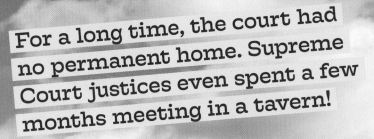
For a long time, the court had no permanent home. Supreme Court justices even spent a few months meeting in a tavern!

The court is housed in the Supreme Court Building in Washington D.C. It is nicknamed the Marble Palace. The building is open to the public. That means you can visit!

Making a Case

You probably know something about courtrooms from television and movies. Two sides have a dispute. They bring their case to a court, with lawyers arguing for both sides. The court then makes a decision about which side is right.

The Supreme Court operates much the same way. But as the highest court in the land, its decisions are important to not just the people involved in the case. The decisions influence every person in the country.

The Highest Court

The United States has several levels of courts. Many lower courts are on the bottom level. Above them are a smaller number of higher courts. At the top, alone, is the Supreme Court.

Imagine you lost a case at a lower, trial court. You could **appeal** to a higher, appeals court. That court might rule in your favor, overturning the lower court's decision. Supreme Court decisions, however, cannot be overturned. There is no higher court to hear an appeal.

Supreme Court

The court system is like a pyramid, with the Supreme Court on top.

Appeals courts, which hear cases that have been decided in lower courts, but appealed

Trial courts, where most cases begin

HOW FUTURE CASES WILL BE DECIDED IF THERE IS A 4-4 TIE

For many months in 2016 and 2017, the Supreme Court had eight rather than nine justices. Having a vacant seat can make it hard for the court to decide cases. Why do you think this is?

Cases and Opinions

The Supreme Court hears many types of cases. Sometimes multiple lower courts issue decisions that interpret the same law very differently. The Supreme Court might then take a case to settle which interpretation is right.

The Supreme Court also hears cases about situations in which rights given by the Constitution are violated. These rights include the right to free speech and to practice the religion of your choice.

To make sure everyone understands their rulings, or decisions, the justices issue opinions. These written documents describe how the justices came to their decision. One justice on the winning side drafts the majority opinion. Sometimes a justice agrees with a ruling, but not for the reasons described in the majority opinion. That justice can write a separate opinion explaining their own reasons. Justices on the losing side can also write opinions to explain why they disagree.

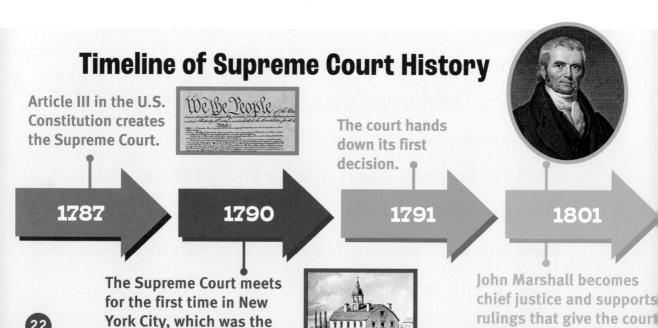

Timeline of Supreme Court History

Article III in the U.S. Constitution creates the Supreme Court.

1787

The Supreme Court meets for the first time in New York City, which was the nation's capital at the time.

1790

The court hands down its first decision.

1791

John Marshall becomes chief justice and supports rulings that give the court more power.

1801

Changing a Decision

When the Supreme Court hands down a decision, it is hard to undo. One way to undo it is for Congress to **amend**, or change, the Constitution. Passing an amendment is difficult, so it rarely happens.

The Supreme Court itself can also change its mind. Justices occasionally conclude that a decision made by an earlier court was wrong. They then take a related case and make a new decision.

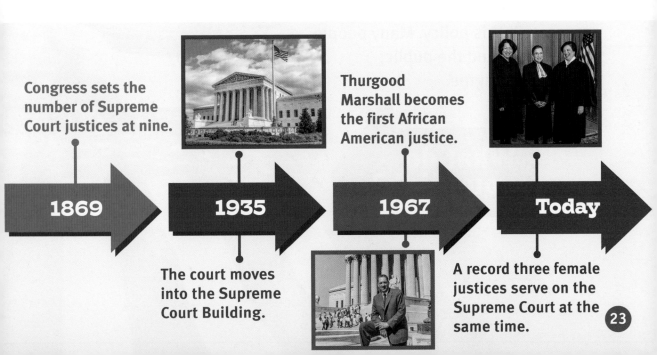

Congress sets the number of Supreme Court justices at nine.

1869

The court moves into the Supreme Court Building.

1935

Thurgood Marshall becomes the first African American justice.

1967

A record three female justices serve on the Supreme Court at the same time.

Today

23

The Court on Camera

Would you like to watch the Supreme Court hear a case? You might be able to if you go to the Supreme Court Building and wait in line for one of the limited visitors' seats. But you can't watch it online or on television. No cameras are allowed in the Supreme Court. Most justices agree with this policy. Many people in the press and the public, however, disagree.

What do you think?

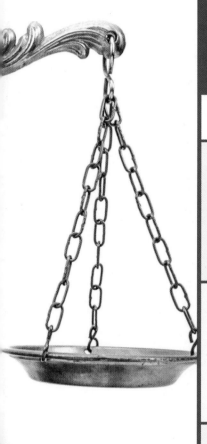

Should people be allowed to take photos and videos of the Supreme Court in action?

YES	NO
✔ Watching the court in action helps educate citizens about how the government works.	✔ Knowing they are on camera could distract lawyers and justices. They may end up worrying more about the public misinterpreting a statement or question than on the quality and honesty of their words.
✔ People would better understand the impact the court has on their lives if they are more familiar with what happens during a case.	✔ Cameras in the courtroom could make the proceedings seem less professional and important.
✔ **Oral**, or spoken, arguments are often important historical events that Americans should be able to see.	✔ Sound recordings of the oral arguments are available online. If people are interested, they can listen to them for free.
✔ The president and members of Congress often appear on television, so the justices should too.	✔ Photos and videos of the justices would make their faces more easily recognizable to the public. This could put the justices' security at risk if someone wanted to threaten or punish them for a decision.

This is the Supreme Court's chamber, where cases are heard. Justices always enter it from behind the red curtain in groups of three.

The justices all shake hands before hearing a case.

The Court at Work

Very few cases ever go all the way to the Supreme Court. The court receives up to 8,000 requests to hear cases each year. But they only hear arguments for about 80 of them. (Go to pages 40 and 41 to read about some of the most important cases in history!) Four of the nine justices have to agree to hear a case. They tend to choose cases that address important legal questions.

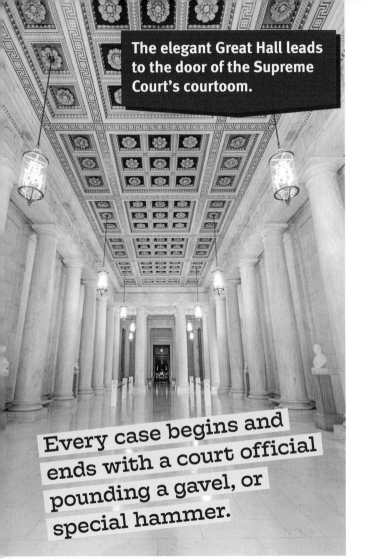

The elegant Great Hall leads to the door of the Supreme Court's courtoom.

Every case begins and ends with a court official pounding a gavel, or special hammer.

Court Is in Session

The Supreme Court is in session only nine months of the year. Each new term begins on the first Monday of October. It usually finishes at the end of June. During each term, the justices switch between about two weeks of sittings and two weeks of recess.

They hear cases or deliver decisions and other announcements to the public in a sitting. During recesses, the justices review cases, debate, and write about their decisions.

Gavels appear in many movies and television shows. But real-life judges rarely use them in the middle of a court hearing. Lawyers and justices follow strict rules about proper behavior during a case. Do you think the judges in this cartoon are following those rules? Why do you think the rules are important?

Arguing Before the Justices

Before the Supreme Court hears a lawsuit, lawyers on both sides write briefs. In these documents, they argue their case. The justices study the briefs. Then in court, they hear the lawyers' oral arguments. The lawyers have only 30 minutes each to explain all their points.

It is an honor to argue a case before the Supreme Court. But it is also challenging. Justices often interrupt the lawyers with questions and comments.

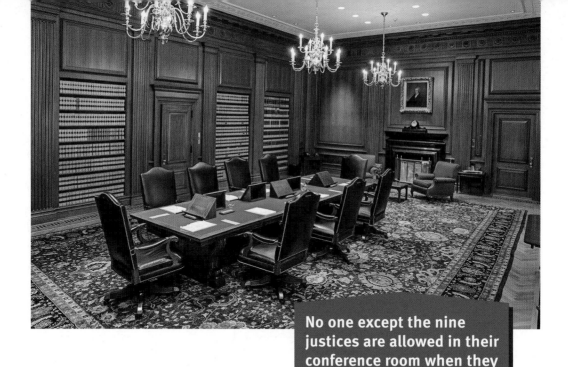

No one except the nine justices are allowed in their conference room when they discuss a case.

Talking It Out

After the oral arguments, the justices meet in a conference room. The chief justice explains how they see the case. Then one at a time, the other justices weigh in. They all try to convince the others to come around to their point of view.

The chief justice then holds a vote. Sometimes everyone agrees, and the decision is **unanimous**. More often, the justices deliver a split decision, and the majority wins.

Flubbing the Oath

Anyone new at a job can be nervous—even a Supreme Court chief justice! In 2009, Chief Justice John Roberts had his first chance to swear in a new president, Barack Obama. But as Roberts recited the oath that Obama was supposed to repeat, he jumbled up the words. To make sure the oath was official, Roberts got a do-over at the White House the next day. This time, he was very careful, making it through the oath with no mistakes.

Barack Obama takes his first oath of office to become president in 2009.

Courting Tradition

The way the Supreme Court conducts its business is guided by old traditions. The judges always wear black robes in court. The robes are modeled after ones worn by British judges before the American Revolution.

British judges also wore white powdered wigs. But this tradition did not catch on in the United States. Many Americans spoke against them, including Thomas Jefferson, who drafted the Declaration of Independence. He described the wigs as "monstrous."

Justice Ruth Bader Ginsburg dresses up her robe with a lacy bib.

Lawyers like to show off the white quills they get from the Supreme Court.

During oral arguments, white quills, or feathers, are set out on the lawyers' tables. Long ago, lawyers dipped the quills' tips into ink and used them as pens. Today, the quills are just souvenirs for the lawyers.

Another tradition involves the newest justice. In the conference room, this justice has to perform humble tasks, such as taking notes and answering the door.

The Supreme Court Building has its own basketball court.

Protesters gather outside the Supreme Court to make their voices heard.

4

You and
the Court

Now you know how the Supreme Court decides cases and how these decisions shape the law of the land. But you still may be wondering exactly what their decisions mean to you. Here are just a few examples of the many ways the Supreme Court makes a difference in your life. You may be surprised to learn that what's familiar to you now came from the court.

Two school girls helped bring the Pledge of Allegiance case to the Supreme Court in 1943.

The Court and Your Classroom

Do you go to a school with kids of different races? The important case *Brown v. Board of Education of Topeka* may be the reason. In this 1954 decision, the court declared it is unconstitutional to make black and white students attend different schools.

Does your class recite the Pledge of Allegiance to the U.S. flag? Because of *West Virginia State Board of Education v. Barnette* in 1943, you can decide whether or not to say the pledge.

Other cases place limits on students' rights. Can teachers **censor** an article you write for a school newspaper? *Hazelwood School District v. Kuhlmeier* from 1988 says they can. How do schools provide what students with disabilities need? *Mills v. Board of Education* helped make sure students with disabilities can attend school and have the services they need. The Supreme Court has also ruled that school officials can search students' backpacks and make students take a drug test if they play sports.

Supreme Court rulings have real-life consequences. Would you want the justices making their decisions in this way?

"Don't spread it around, but on the really tough ones, I just go with 'eenie, meenie, minie, moe.'"

Placing Limits

The Supreme Court affects your life outside of school too. Because of *United States v. Darby* in 1941, Congress can limit how many hours a week a child can work.

Kent v. United States in 1966 established the process for trying some **juvenile** offenders as adults rather than as children. If found guilty, these young offenders can receive harsh punishments, including life in prison.

Some kids used to work up to 18 hours a day.

The government can block you from looking at some websites. Do you think this is fair?

Some cases have dealt with computers. One was *United States v. American Library Assn., Inc.* in 2003. The court ruled that the government could keep you from seeing certain websites in public libraries.

Each year, the Supreme Court hears new cases on new issues. Perhaps you will play a part in a case that goes all the way to the Supreme Court! Who knows?

Some Important Supreme Court Cases

Here are some Supreme Court cases whose decisions have had major effects on life in the United States.

1800

1900

Loving v. Virginia
Year: 1967

Effect: States have to allow people of different races to marry one another.

McCulloch v. Maryland
Year: 1819

Effect: The federal government has more power than the Constitution specifically says.

Miranda v. Arizona
Year: 1966

Effect: Before questioning suspects, police must explain that they have a right to remain silent and to have a lawyer.

Brown v. Board of Education
Year: 1954

Effect: States cannot create segregated schools.

Marbury v. Madison
Year: 1803

Effect: The Supreme Court helped secure a right to strike down laws it deems unconstitutional.

Bush v. Gore

Year: 2000

Effect: George W. Bush became president. All efforts to recount the votes in the 2000 presidential election ended.

2000

District of Columbia v. Heller

Year: 2008

Effect: Americans have a right to own guns to defend themselves.

Citizens United v. Federal Election Commission

Year: 2010

Effect: Corporations can spend money to discuss campaign issues, as long as the money does not go directly to a candidate.

The News

H COURT BANS
REGATION IN
BLIC SCHOOLS

JOE CHARGES
'IRON CURTAIN'

Speaking Out Against the Vietnam War

In the 1960s, students took a case all they way to the Supreme Court to defend their rights.

On December 16, 1965, 13-year-old Mary Beth Tinker wore a black band of cloth around her arm to school. The armband was part of a protest she had organized. She and other students wore them to speak out against the Vietnam War (1954–1975). Mary Beth did not think it was right that young soldiers were being drafted into, or forced to serve in, the military and dying in the war.

Mary Beth (left) stands with her brother. The symbol on their armbands stands for "peace."

Children also marched in protests against the Vietnam War.

Her school punished the protesters. They were suspended and not allowed to return until after Christmas.

Mary Beth, her brother John, and another student fought back. With their parents' support, they filed a lawsuit against the school. The kids claimed the school had violated their right to free speech.

In 1969, the case came before the Supreme Court. In a 7–2 decision, the court ruled that public schools can't censor what students say. If you ever wear a political T-shirt to class, you can thank Mary Beth Tinker.

Get Involved!

The Supreme Court is supposed to work for you. But you still have a role in our system. Here are a few steps you can take to be a good citizen:

Read and watch the news. Learn about Supreme Court cases and the issues they address.

Talk with your friends about changes you would like to see in your community.

Ask your parents to take you to protests that address causes you believe in.

Watch the Senate confirmation hearing when a new Supreme Court justice is nominated. Would the nominee be a good addition to the court?

Tour the Supreme Court Building if you're ever able to visit Washington, D.C. If the court is in session, you might be lucky enough to see the justices in action!

Did you find the truth?

(T) **The president could nominate a kid to serve on the Supreme Court.**

(F) **The first female justice joined the Supreme Court in 1906.**

Resources

The book you just read is a first introduction to the Supreme Court, and to the history and government of our country. There is always more to learn and discover. In addition to this title, we encourage you to seek out complementary resources.

Other books in this series:

 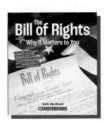 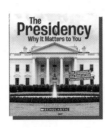  

You can also look at:

Benoit, Peter. *Supreme Court*. New York: Children's Press, 2014.

Kemp, Kristin. *Amazing Americans: Thurgood Marshall*. Huntington Beach, CA: Teacher Created Materials, 2015.

Sotomayor, Sonia. *The Beloved World of Sonia Sotomayor*. New York: Delacorte Books for Young Readers, 2018.

Stoltman, Joan. *20 Fun Facts About the Supreme Court*. New York: Gareth Stevens Publishing, 2018.

Winter, Jonah. *Ruth Bader Ginsburg: The Case of R.B.G vs. Inequality*. New York: Abrams Books for Young Readers, 2017.

Glossary

amend (uh-MEND) to change a legal document or a law

appeal (uh-PEEL) to apply to a higher court for a change in a legal decision

censor (SEN-sur) to remove parts of a book, movie, or other work that are thought to be unacceptable or offensive

federal (FED-ur-uhl) national; describing a system of government in which states are united under a central authority

impeachment (im-PEECH-ment) bringing formal charges against a public official

justices (JUHS-tis-ez) judges on the Supreme Court

juvenile (JOO-vuh-nuhl) relating to a person who is under 18 years of age

nominates (NAH-muh-nates) suggests that someone would be a good person to do an important job or to receive an honor

oral (OR-uhl) spoken instead of written

republic (ri-PUHN-lik) a form of government in which the people have the power to elect representatives who manage the government

unanimous (yoo-NAN-uh-muhs) agreed on by everyone

unconstitutional (uhn-kahn-stih-TOO-shuh-nuhl) not in keeping with the basic principles or laws set forth in the constitution of a state or country

Index

Page numbers in **bold** indicate illustrations.

About the Author

A graduate of Swarthmore College, Liz Sonneborn lives in Brooklyn, New York. She is the author of more than 100 books, most for young readers. She often writes about American history, world history, and biography. Her books include *The United States Constitution*, *The Pledge of Allegiance*, *The Star-Spangled Banner*, and *Miranda v. Arizona*. Sonneborn has also contributed to *Supreme Court Justices: A Biographical Dictionary*.